Original title:
The Banana Grove

Copyright © 2025 Creative Arts Management OÜ
All rights reserved.

Author: Kieran Blackwood
ISBN HARDBACK: 978-1-80586-450-9
ISBN PAPERBACK: 978-1-80586-922-1

Fields of Fun

In the shade of green, where monkeys swing,
Bananas hang low, it's a fruity thing.
Chasing the yellow with laughter and cheer,
Jokes flying 'round as we munch and peer.

Feet slipping on peels, a classic mistake,
Giggles erupt with each little quake.
Who knew a fruit could bring such delight?
As we tumble and roll, what a comical sight!

The sun sets low, painting skies so bright,
Dancing with shadows, what a funny sight.
With friends all around, the jokes never end,
In this wacky patch, we're all on the mend.

Banana splits race, who will take the crown?
With cream and a cherry, we all gather 'round.
Life's full of laughter in this sunny clime,
Join us again, for a merry good time!

Dreams of a Sunlit Retreat

Under yellow hats they scheme,
Bouncing on a sunlit beam.
Swinging low, they tease the breeze,
Hanging out in leafy ease.

With antics that never quit,
Joking in a rhythmic fit.
They play games beyond the norm,
Where laughter dances, bright and warm.

Serenity in the Shade

In silken shadows, time stands still,
Sipping juice from nature's thrill.
With friends close by, the giggles rise,
As fluffy clouds float through blue skies.

Banana peels become a slide,
Where silly giggles can't subside.
Lazing low, they roll and spin,
In this haven, joy begins.

Pathways of Sweetness

Through the grove, a trail unfolds,
Sticky fingers, stories told.
Every twist, a comical sight,
As fruit flies dance in pure delight.

Chasing tails of plucky glee,
Crack open smiles, don't you see?
Underneath the dancing leaves,
Life's a joke that never leaves.

Embrace of the Luscious Landscape

In a place where giggles grow,
Joy blooms brightly, don't you know?
With every fruit a playful jest,
In this paradise, we find our best.

Laughter echoes in every nook,
As we gather, let's share a hook.
With a wink, they swing and sway,
In the sun, they're here to play.

Enchanted Edges

In the land where monkeys swing,
The gossip flies on a banana string.
Chasing curls of playful peels,
With giggles that no one conceals.

The critters dance in leafy cheer,
Climbing high, with nary a fear.
A tickle here, a silly slip,
Who knew fruit could make you trip?

The chattering birds join the fun,
Making music beneath the sun.
A laughing lizard steals the show,
Swiveling its tail, dancing slow.

Harmony of the Residents

A parrot squawks in joyous tune,
While ants march on under the moon.
Squirrels leap with a cheeky grin,
In this harmony, we all fit in.

The raccoons wear a mask of glee,
Playing hide and seek by the tree.
Each critter shares a wacky tale,
As the evening wind begins to wail.

In this grove, no one's alone,
Each laughter shared brings love that's grown.
From cheeky chimps to silly snakes,
Together here, the heart awakes.

Aromas of Autumn's Kiss

Splashes of yellow with orange bright,
The scent of fun fills the cool night.
Bouncing bugs and wiggly worms,
Flavors of laughter swirl in terms.

As harvests fall with a crunchy sound,
Unexpected pranks can still be found.
The pumpkins giggle while they roll,
Tickled by breezes, hearts feel whole.

Every twilight brings a feast,
With tales of jests that never ceased.
The squirrels snatch bites of pies,
While moonlight dances in their eyes.

Green Palettes and Golden Hues

In this patch where colors blend,
Each leaf a canvass, none can pretend.
Lush greens laugh with golden gleams,
Nature's joke is bursting at the seams.

The sunbeams tickle, shadows play,
Dancing colors lit by the day.
With every breeze, a joke takes flight,
Bouncing echoes into the night.

Bumblebees buzz with cheeky flair,
Pollen parties in the air.
A vibrant prankster's sweet perfume,
Invites us all to join and bloom.

Songs of the Swaying Branches

In a land where silliness thrives,
Bouncing fruit like jolly lives,
Branches wiggle, with glee they dance,
Each wave and nod, a fruit-filled prance.

Silly shadows cast a show,
Beneath the glow, all laughs grow,
Chasing critters in the breeze,
Laughter ripples through the trees.

Mirth Among the Fruiting Allies

In bright attire, the fruits convene,
Chatting whimsically, quite the scene,
Bantering sweet as candy rain,
Snack-time giggles, never pain.

The pudding cups of sassy lore,
Watch the buzz like never before,
Mashed and mixed, a giggling spree,
A feast of fruits, wild jubilee!

Fatigued Leaves

Leaves droop down, feeling quite spent,
Whispering tales of joy well-bent,
Taking a break from their hard work,
With dreams of summer, laughter's perk.

They complain of games, lost in the breeze,
Yet still take part with lazy ease,
A leafy sigh, a chuckle low,
Life's a gamble, just let it flow!

Fruity Dreams

In a world where dreams are bright,
Fruity friends have late-night flight,
Bouncing high on sugary clouds,
Singing softly, laughing loud.

With twinkle lights of lemon cheer,
A grand parade of giggles near,
All together, wild and free,
In a fruity dream, just you and me!

The Melodies of Mellow Yellow

Banana bands strum tunes of fun,
Bouncing beats, they've just begun,
Echoing joy through leafy halls,
With each cheer, the laughter calls.

Dancing peels in rhythmic sway,
Twirling fruits in grand display,
Colors bright, a giggling crew,
In melodies where dreams come true!

Burgeoning Bliss Bliss

In a corner of the land, they sway,
Bright yellow munchies, come what may.
They tickle the breeze with giggles galore,
These sunny fruits, always wanting more.

A monkey named Lou swings in the trees,
Tickling each bunch, shouting with glee.
He juggles the fruit, oh what a sight,
While birds in the air join in his delight.

They wear little hats, such splendid attire,
Balancing fruits like it's a grand choir.
Who knew that a peel could bring such cheer?
In this silly grove, the fun's crystal clear!

So grab your fork and join in the fun,
These fruity delights are never outdone.
With laughter and joy, we dance and we sing,
In the land of the yellow, let happiness spring.

Spheres of Sunshine

In a bright patch of laughter, fruits sway high,
With a wink and a smile, they flirt with the sky.
Each yellow orb sports a cheeky grin,
Promising sweetness beneath their thin skin.

A parrot named Pete starts a fruity parade,
With dancing and singing, the fun never fades.
They twist and they turn in the gleeful daylight,
Making this grove a pure delight!

Spheres of sunshine with stories to tell,
Each one a jester, casting a spell.
With squeaky voices, they burst into song,
In this nutty grove, you can't go wrong!

The squirrels join in, with their frolicsome flair,
Doing the limbo without any care.
So join the jollity, join the delight,
In this zany expanse, everything feels right!

Visions of Verdant Freedom

Beneath a canopy of joy, they dangle free,
Whispering secrets, just you and me.
These fellows have tales of sun and of fun,
In their leafy kingdom, there's never a pun!

A curious sloth peeks out from his seat,
Balancing fruits, what a whimsical feat!
With each careful move, he's a real fruit star,
Drawing laughs as he slips—oh, there goes a jar!

They roll in the grass, bumping with glee,
These yellow delights are as silly as can be.
In this playful realm where the wild things bloom,
Every fruity moment dispels all the gloom!

So come take a trip to where laughter stems,
In the land of the happy, we're all best friends.
With visions of freedom, our spirits will soar,
In this funny world, who could ask for more?

Harvesting Joy at Dawn

As the sun rises mildly, a glittering show,
Golden delights greet the day with a glow.
They wiggle and jiggle in morning's first light,
Sipping on dew drops, oh what a sight!

A rowdy raccoon is ready to play,
He's built a grand tower of fruits for the day.
With laughter erupting and cheers in the air,
This morning is bursting with whimsical flair!

Each fruity treasure calls out from its perch,
Inviting you in for a jovial search.
With giggles and wiggles, adventures unfold,
Harvesting happiness worth more than gold!

So grab a friend, come dance in the morn,
In this silly gathering, joyful hearts are born.
With laughter at dawn, let the day sprout anew,
In this cheerful patch, there's always room for two!

Celebrations of Seasonal Splendor

Yellow bunches hang with glee,
Dancing lightly, wild and free.
Silly monkeys swing around,
On their laughter, joy is found.

Picnic snacks in piles so bright,
Food fights during the day and night.
Frisbees fly and laughter roars,
Underneath the playful shores.

People trip and giggle loud,
As they bounce and form a crowd.
Sticky fingers, smiles so wide,
On this fun-filled, sunny ride.

Jumpy feet on squishy ground,
In this place, pure joy is found.
Every season, share a cheer,
Celebrate the laughs, my dear.

Sunshine's Lullaby

Wiggly worms tumble and play,
As bright sun sends the clouds away.
Leaves chuckle, dancing in the breeze,
Tickled toes, oh how they tease!

A splash of juice drips on the floor,
Juicy smiles are worth much more.
Bumblebees buzz a silly tune,
While kids leap like it's noon!

Chasing shadows, playful race,
Frogs croak their sweet embrace.
Under the shade, tales unfold,
Of giggles, pranks, and laughter bold.

The sun will dip, but not our fun,
With every giggle, adventures run.
As daylight fades and dreams arise,
Lullabies of joy fill the skies.

A Pilgrimage of Treetops

Join the climb to heights so sweet,
Where sneaky squirrels play and greet.
Up they go, with acrobat flair,
Balancing stunts hanging in the air!

Branches wave like friendly hands,
Cheering on the monkey bands.
Nuts for everyone, sweet delights,
Feasting under the twinkling lights.

Leaping down with bold delight,
Splat! You land, what a sight!
Covered in leaves, you laugh and cheer,
As nature whispers, "Don't you fear!"

Homeward bound with shirt askew,
Tales of trees and skies so blue.
From the heights where joy takes flight,
Adventure's glow, both day and night.

Blooms of the Happy Harvest

Gather 'round for a fruity feast,
Where silliness never seems to cease.
Pies and treats, so bright and round,
Joyful moments, love abound!

Colors pop, the table's set,
Sticky fingers, no regrets.
Laughter crashes like waves on shore,
Every giggle opens a door.

Tummies ache, but hearts are full,
As we roll and dance, hear the pull.
With every bite, the world feels right,
Under the stars, shining bright.

Though seasons change and days go fast,
Our silly times are meant to last.
Harvest memories, hold them tight,
In the warmth of laughter's light.

Sweetness in the Shade

In a grove where the sun shines bright,
Monkeys swing left and right.
With peels that dance in the breeze,
A fruit parade with joyful ease.

They jest and giggle, oh what a sight,
Chasing shadows in delight.
Bananas launch from the trees,
Falling down like playful leaves.

A bunch so silly, they take a bow,
Grinning bright as they plop down now.
The laughter echoes through the air,
Sweetness bursting everywhere!

In this place of golden glee,
You'd think a fruit party was meant to be.
With every slip and every fall,
It's pure fun for one and all!

Laughter of the Yellow Fruit

A cluster of smiles wrapped in yellow,
They chatter, they tumble, oh what a fellow!
In this fruity circus, joy takes flight,
Each one with its own comic height.

One slips and slides, what a blunder,
Hilarity sparks like playful thunder.
Bouncing off branches, they join the fray,
Squeezing out laughs the silly way.

With every peel comes a cackle and cheer,
These drop-dead jokers have no fear.
A comedic show, ripe with zest,
In this fruity laughter, they are blessed.

So here in this quirky, sunny space,
The yellow fellows find their place.
With every giggle, they thrive on fun,
In this vibrant world, they've surely won!

Underneath the Waving Palms

Beneath the palms that wave and sway,
Fruity laughter fills the day.
A bunch of gigglers in a line,
Taking turns at silly mime.

One juggles fruit with quite the flair,
While others watch, they're unaware.
A slip, a flop, then fits of glee,
The sweetest circus, wild and free!

They roll and bounce along the ground,
With every fall, they're joy unbound.
Chasing shadows, seeking the light,
What a show, pure delight!

Amongst the laughter and sunny rays,
These silly fruits ignite the days.
In this shade where fun ignites,
They dance and sing through joyful nights!

Sonic Serenade of the Understory

Beneath the leaves, the drumming starts,
With squishy sounds and fruity arts.
A serenade of laughter plays,
In this leafy realm, we spend our days.

With every thud, a chuckle flows,
Bananas burst out in comic shows.
The rhythms of joy rise up like steam,
Turning simple moments into a dream.

Floppy peels make the perfect drum,
A fruity beat makes everyone hum.
Twisting and turning in the green,
The silliest moments ever seen!

So here in this vibrant, fruity land,
Where laughter plays on nature's hand,
The melody of fun forever sings,
A symphony that only sweetness brings!

The Grove's Gentle Embrace

In the shade, where laughter grows,
Monkeys swing with silly toes.
Peels slide off with giggles loud,
Dancing feet in happiness proud.

Sunshine spills like spilled juice,
Bright and cheery, no excuse.
Chasing tails and playful pranks,
Bouncing joy in leafy ranks.

Here the yo-yos spin around,
With every plop, a funny sound.
Laughter echoes through the trees,
As giggling birds fluff in the breeze.

Bunches hanging, ripe and sweet,
Tripping kids run with swift feet.
In this place, we're young and bold,
Stories of fun are always told.

Chronicles of Curved Delight

In a land where curves abound,
Banana boats are soon to be found.
With sails of leaves and peels to grasp,
We ride the waves with giddy gasp.

Sailing past the baked potato,
Played by birds, oh, what a show!
Quacking ducks with fruit-filled dreams,
Chasing clouds with silly schemes.

Each curve leads to laughter deep,
While monkeys leap and seldom sleep.
Tales of slips and banana slides,
In the sun, our joy abides.

Curvy paths that twist like smiles,
Where fun is found in endless miles.
Oh, what a ride, it's just a tease,
In this land of leafy ease.

Harbingers of Harvest

When harvest moon begins to shine,
The party starts with fruit so fine.
Juggling peels and tossing fun,
Laughs erupt until we're done.

Green bananas play hide and seek,
While sneaky squirrels plan a sneak.
A game of chase, round and round,
In this fun-filled, fruity ground.

Every giggle pulls a whiff,
Of ripe delight—a tasty gift.
Bananas dance in merry rows,
As laughter through the garden flows.

Harvest time brings joy and cheer,
With every slip, there's naught to fear.
So join the fun, don't hesitate,
In this fruity place, it's simply great!

Swaying in the Summer Breeze

In the breeze, the leaves do sway,
Crafting fun in a cheeky play.
Sunshine tickles our carefree toes,
As giggles flow like rivers close.

Each swing creates a merry song,
Where everyone can tag along.
With laughter bright as golden rays,
We dance beneath the fruited maze.

Silly pranks like flying pies,
Make a mess and roll our eyes.
In this place, mishaps are fine,
As we all munch on fruit divine.

The summer breeze whispers a tale,
Of wobbly rides and fruity scale.
So come along, let's all be free,
In this joyful jubilee!

Arcadian Encounters

In a grove where laughter grows,
Bananas dance in playful rows.
Monkeys swing from branch to branch,
While squirrels put on a tiny ranch.

Picnics with peels piled high,
Dandelion hats that make us fly.
Everyone slips in a fruit-filled spree,
Giggles echo, wild and free.

Chasing shadows, we take a chance,
Gorillas join in a silly dance.
Each twist and turn, a fruity thrill,
With every note, the glee we spill.

Sunshine smiles as we play our game,
Even the plants seem to share our name.
In this haven of zany sights,
Every hour is wrapped in delights.

Palms and Plentiful Produce

Under palms, the treasures lay,
Golden fruit in bright array.
A pitfall here, a peel slips there,
Laughter bounces in the air.

Swaying vines invite to play,
While critters munch throughout the day.
Chirping birds join in our cheer,
Making this place one we hold dear.

We'll juggle fruit, a silly feat,
As neighbors meet for a fruity treat.
Who knew life could feel so spry,
With fruity fun that never runs dry?

Under starry skies, we dare,
To laugh and dance without a care.
In this realm of sun and shade,
Monty Python would be amazed!

Tales from a Leafy Paradise

In the shade of palm fronds wide,
Funny tales of fruit reside.
A chef who dropped his banana pie,
Caused laughter that made sparrows sigh.

A silly frog in a peel boat,
Floated by with a comical note.
'Tis not the sun, but joy we fear,
And slip on our jokes throughout the year.

The monkeys debate on fashion trends,
In hats made of leaves, the fun never ends.
With every joke, the laughter grows,
As wild stories fill the prose.

In this haven where humor thrives,
Even the fruit seems to have lives.
With quirky moments we hold dear,
A fruit-filled world that sings with cheer.

Glimmers of Golden Days

Golden rays through leaf and vine,
Silly creatures sip on brine.
A parrot cracks the silliest joke,
While giggling worms around us poke.

Sunny mischief fills the air,
As fruits tumble in a sweet despair.
We partake in a friendly race,
In this grove, we find our place.

Wobbling squirrels bring the noise,
They flaunt their gathering, oh what poise!
Beneath the canopy so dense,
Life's a laugh, it makes perfect sense.

With every nibble and playful shout,
Joy is what life's really about.
In this land where fun's in play,
We cherish each silly golden day.

The Dance of Devotion

In yellow hats they sway with glee,
A fruity jig beneath a tree.
With peel in hand, they take the lead,
Oh, watch them dance, it's quite the breed!

Nutty laughter fills the air,
They slip and slide without a care.
Elvis tunes make branches shake,
Even squirrels begin to quake!

Their moves are silly, quite absurd,
A chorus of the chirpy bird.
Around and round in joyous loops,
'Round giant fruits, they form their troops!

The sight's a joy, a grand parade,
In this grove, no one's afraid.
So join the fun, don't be a bore,
Let's dance and sing, forevermore!

Oasis of Juicy Joy

A sunny patch where laughter grows,
With every breeze, a tickle blows.
The fruits are ripe, a sight to see,
In this oasis, we all agree!

The munching bandits swing and sway,
Bananas laugh; they're here to play.
With faces sticky, and smiles wide,
Who won the race? No need to hide!

The juice runs down in rivers sweet,
And every nibble is a treat.
Chasing friends beneath the sun,
The best of times, for everyone!

With giggles loud, we roam around,
In this haven, joy is found.
So grab a bunch and join the spree,
For life is grand, we all agree!

Journey to the Golden Heart

Come along, let's take a ride,
On this path of fruits and pride.
With sunshine bright and giggles free,
We'll find the heart, just you and me!

The twirling vines call out our names,
Where everyone forgets their shames.
Oh to frolic, oh to leap,
In golden dreams, our treasures heap!

From lofty heights, we spy our prize,
A fruity feast, it's no surprise.
We'll make a toast with goofy grins,
A party starts, let fun begin!

With joyful hearts, we'll sing aloud,
In this playground, we feel proud.
So come, my friend, let's not depart,
Together here, we'll seek the heart!

Tranquility in the Tender Grove

Among soft leaves, the laughter rings,
As bustling bees hum while joy swings.
With every taste, a giggle flies,
Beneath the shade, the fun never dies!

The gentle breeze adds to the fun,
With every munch, we're overrun.
A tender spot where silliness grows,
A little wildness, who really knows?

The hammock sways, the fruits parade,
In this haven, we're not afraid.
Jokes are shared, and stories unfold,
In this sweet nook, the magic's bold!

So lay down here, embrace the cheer,
In this sweet grove, we'll persevere.
With friends by side, we'll make it last,
A chuckle here, a giggle fast!

Memories in a Tropical Breeze

In the shade where laughter roams,
Chasing monkeys, dodging gnomes.
With peels slipping, giggles spill,
Tropical mischief gives a thrill.

Wacky hats and sunny skies,
Silly games, no need for lies.
Jumps and tumbles, oh what fun,
Underneath the golden sun.

A slip, a slide, a joyful screech,
Every day, a new fun reach.
So many friends, with hearts so light,
A foolish dance that feels just right.

Memories made in vibrant hues,
Colorful skies, and joyful views.
With every laugh, a story told,
In a place where youth is bold.

Threads of Gold in Green Expanse.

Where leafy laughter intertwines,
Golden threads on swaying vines.
Hats askew, we dance around,
Each twirl, a new joy found.

In this patch, we paint the day,
With every step in goofy play.
A fruit parade runs wild and free,
Who knew bananas could be glee?

Chasing critters, dodging spills,
Every day brings new cheap thrills.
With ripe treasures hanging high,
We reach up, attempting to fly.

Sticky fingers and happy grins,
Sharing tales as laughter spins.
In this jungle, fun won't cease,
We find our silly inner peace.

Whispers of Golden Fruit

In the trees, a soft hiss calls,
Golden treasures behind green walls.
Giggling friends with peels so ripe,
We're bumping into funny hype.

A sudden slip, a wobble too,
Oops! There goes my hat askew.
Rolling laughter on the ground,
In this chaos, fun is found.

Monkey business fills the air,
Chasing fruits without a care.
Underneath the dancing beams,
Every moment bursts with dreams.

With every munch, a chuckle shared,
Sweetened joy, fully prepared.
In this orchard, wild and bright,
We spin and twirl into the night.

Echoes in the Canopy

Through the green, the echoes bounce,
Banana peels give joy a pounce.
Friends unite in playful schemes,
Laughter dances, bubbles dreams.

Dodging laughter in the breeze,
Climbing trees with effortless ease.
All around, a splendid mess,
Banana hat? Add some finesse!

Bouncing sounds of joy resound,
In this grove, treasure is found.
With each twist and every cheer,
Funny whispers fill the sphere.

As the sun begins to fade,
We recount all the fun we made.
With memories stitched in playful tones,
This silly space feels like home.

Kindred Spirits of the Green Realm

In the shade where laughter grows,
Silly squirrels strike silly poses.
A chattering troop on a leafy spree,
Swinging high, oh what glee!

Bananas dangling, a golden crown,
Frogs in tuxedos hop up and down.
Our leafy friends tell tales so bold,
Of treasure hunts where jokes unfold.

With each jiggle of the vine,
A comic twist serves as the sign.
They all break out in rhythmic cheer,
As the sun dips low, it's finally clear.

So grab a joke and join the crew,
For in this realm, there's fun for you!
Laughter echoes, a flying kite,
In the green realm, we feel just right.

Secrets Beneath the Canopy

Whispers tickle the leafy stage,
Where critters plot and outsmart the sage.
A parrot's riddle, a monkey's grin,
Unraveling secrets where tales begin.

Twirling spiders spin webs of jest,
While a bumblebee puts humor to the test.
Ticklish branches sway left and right,
Echoing giggles all through the night.

A turtle wearing a tiny hat,
Scratches its shell, 'Oh, where's my cat?'
And though it's clear there's no fluffed fur,
The laughter spreads, oh how it stirs!

So trod on paths softer than fluff,
For in this grove, it's more than enough.
Laughter's the treasure buried deep down,
Join us here, no sign of a frown.

Dance of the Tropical Nights

Beneath the stars, the leaves do sway,
Critters gather for a party play.
Chirps and hisses start the show,
With dance moves that make the moon glow.

Cockatoos croon in goofy tunes,
While raccoons tumble beneath the moons.
The night is young, the groove is strong,
As laughter bursts like bubbles along.

Fireflies twinkle, a glowing line,
To guide the crowd in a conga line.
With jingling fruits and goofy hops,
The sounds of joy never stop!

So come along, put on your shoes,
Join the fest where nobody snoozes.
The melody twirls with a cheeky bite,
In this nighttime bash, everything feels right.

The Prowling Monkeys' Jamboree

On branches high, the jesters swing,
With giggles low, they leap and cling.
From nuts to pranks, they plot a spree,
A curious chase, a wild jubilee.

With cheeky faces and playful eyes,
They toss around fun with no goodbyes.
A stolen snack leads to a race,
Laughing loudly, they embrace the chase.

Bouncing berries, a feast so grand,
Their finger painting with banana band.
Art with humor all around,
In this playful realm, joy will abound.

So join the march for cheers galore,
With prancing feet, we holler for more.
United in laughter, we'll surely see,
The joy that thrives in our jubilee!

Nature's Golden Embrace

In the trees, a jiggle and sway,
Yellow smiles beam through the day.
Monkeys swing with gleeful cheer,
Peeling laughter fills the air near.

A fruit parade, a slippery race,
One misstep, what a silly face!
The ground's a stage for playful pranks,
As nature's jesters give their thanks.

Bunches partying in the sun,
A fruit-filled world that's so much fun.
With every bite, a giggle shared,
In this grove, nothing's compared.

Nature's treasure, oh what a sight,
Frolicsome sunbeams shining bright.
In every corner, smiles do bloom,
A joyful echo in this room.

Sun-Kissed Whispers of the Past

Once upon a time, in leafy tales,
Giggling fruits danced like happy snails.
Whispers travel through the breeze,
Tickling branches and buzzing bees.

With every twirl, a tale unfolds,
Of slippery monkeys and brave young molds.
Chasing shadows, racing the light,
In this grove, everything feels right.

The golden globes, they sway and tease,
Jokesters of nature among the trees.
Old tales linger, wrapped in gold,
As laughter's stories continue to mold.

Memories hanging like ripe fruit,
With every laugh, roots grow deep in truth.
In this haven where whims do blend,
Sun-kissed whispers are the best friend.

Delights Wrapped in Nature's Cloak

Under the canopy, funny sights,
Laughter erupting on sunny heights.
Fruits wear hats of polka dots,
During the day, they spin their plots.

Nature's cloak in shades of green,
Harbors giggles yet unseen.
A bunch of mischief up in the air,
With antics that would give you a scare!

Dancing shadows and gleeful cries,
As golden delights wave goodbye.
The charm of play is never shy,
Silly surprises come fluttering by.

Each bite is sweet, a flavor burst,
Filling our hearts with nature's thirst.
Wrapped in joy, we sing aloud,
Together we stand, forever proud.

Journey Through the Jungle Orchard

Hop aboard the giggle train,
Chugging through this leafy lane.
Sunshine tickles all around,
While fruit confetti rains down.

Monkeys drop in for a laugh,
Their silly tricks are the best half.
In this orchard, fun's the game,
Every moment's never the same.

Bananarama, what a sight,
A twisty dance, pure delight!
The jungle sky paints shades of cheer,
As we gather smiles, far and near.

Adventure waits, so come and play,
With fruit-filled joy, let's seize the day!
In the orchard where laughter reigns,
Together we'll dance through sun and rains.

Fruity Fantasies Untold

In a land where monkeys dance,
Bananas lead the wild romance.
Peels slip under happy feet,
Fruits conspire, oh what a treat!

Sunlight glimmers on the skin,
As laughter joins the leafy din.
Caught in vines, the giggles grow,
Nature's jokes in a circus show.

Silly squirrels wear hats so grand,
With fruit cups carefully planned.
Misfit critters form a crew,
Turning fruits into a zoo!

In this jungle, fun's the key,
With playful snacks, come join the spree.
Fruity dreams are here to stay,
A jolly feast awaits today!

Serenade of the Sun-Kissed

Underneath the golden rays,
Fragrant fun begins to blaze.
Pineapples sing in harmony,
While coconuts join the symphony.

Bouncing fruits in joyful glee,
Tickle the air, oh can't you see?
Laughter echoes through the trees,
As mangoes dance in the breeze.

Bananas sport their polka dots,
Making friends with silly knots.
A party hosted by the vine,
Each bite brings a fruity shine.

With every giggle, spirits soar,
In this grove, there's always more.
Come along, friends, take a chance,
Join the fruit and make a dance!

Tropical Reverie

In the shade of leafy crowns,
Limes and lemons wear their frowns.
But in the sun, they get so bright,
Turning sour into pure delight!

Papayas strut with confidence,
With each juicy drop, they commence.
Grapes giggle in clusters tight,
Unexpected turns make pure delight.

Pluck a berry, hear it squeal,
Amidst the fun, it's quite the deal.
Honeyed whispers fill the glen,
Fruitful secrets shared by friends.

In this realm where laughter grows,
Beneath the trees, the humor flows.
Let's embrace the fruity cheer,
In this paradise, leave your fear!

Nectar of Nature's Bounty

Ripe and ready on the vine,
Fruitful whims and silly lines.
Laughter bubbles up like juice,
In this grove, we set it loose!

Oranges juggle with delight,
While lemons take to glorious flight.
Kiwi winks with playful flair,
Creating bubbles in the air.

Bananas swing with gleeful ease,
They prance about in a gentle breeze.
With every peel, a chuckle spreads,
As nature laughs, no need for beds.

So come and share this fruity dance,
Where every bite invites a chance.
In this land of endless glee,
Nature's bounty sets us free!

Conversations Under Canopies

In the shade of bright green leaves,
Monkeys chatter, doubling beliefs.
One says bananas taste like foam,
While the other claims they're not from home.

A parrot squawks, calling for snacks,
While squirrels debate on sneaky tracks.
The breeze laughs, rustling the fronds,
As jokes fly like a chorus of wands.

Giggling and grinning, they share their tales,
Of fruit-flavored pranks and mischievous gales.
In this lively grove, no secrets stay,
Every fruit's story gets a grand play!

They dance on vines, a clumsy parade,
Spinning in circles, their energy displayed.
In this fruity world, they live with glee,
Who knew a calm grove could house such spree?

Heartbeats of the Tropical Thicket

In the heart of the grove, odd sounds arise,
Like bananas giggling under sunny skies.
A lizard in bow ties takes a quick spin,
While crickets hum tunes, winning the din.

Fruits play poker, their stakes are high,
"Ripe or not?" the ripe ones cry.
A mango fluffs up, tries to bluff,
While a shy coconut says, "This is tough!"

Beneath tangled roots, the laughter's free,
With a parrot planner, plotting spree.
"Let's have a feast!" he squawks with delight,
As he paints the scene in sheer delight!

And so they share under the wide blue dome,
In this laughter-filled and fruity home.
With twinkling eyes, they boast and cheer,
In every heartbeat, joy is near!

The Mystique of Sundrenched Splendor

In sunlit corners where textures meet,
Fruits spin tales with quickened heartbeat.
Bananas in hats, prancing about,
Throwing confetti with zest, no doubt!

The breeze carries whispers of playful tunes,
Bouncing off branches like joyful balloons.
In pajamas, a fig sings, "Join my crew!"
While pineapples dance, giggling, "How do you do?"

A walrus strolls in, with smoothies to share,
But slips on a peel—oh, what a scare!
He rolls down the slope, with laughter galore,
While everyone cheers and shouts, "More! More!"

Amidst the fun, a wild rhythm sways,
As laughter explodes in bright, sunny rays.
With joy unyielding, their spirits soar free,
Under splendor where mischief's the key!

Odyssey of the Orchard

A journey unfolds in this fruity domain,
Where bananas don capes, escaping the plain.
They swing from branches, daring the fate,
In a quest for the grandest, the biggest plate!

Peaches plot schemes amid shadows of green,
While watermelons dance, ever so keen.
"Let's have a party!" the apples do shout,
"Bring all your quirks, leave your worries out!"

Berries boost tunes with a jive and a skip,
While mangoes narrate with flavor-filled quips.
Their banquet awaits under twinkling bright,
As laughter and stories ignite the night.

In this whirlpool of fruits, friendship blooms,
As oranges juggle, bantering their dooms.
And a cheerful chorus sings in the air,
In this orchard adventure, joy is everywhere!

Vibrance Among the Groves

In a place where the colors clash,
Fruits wear smiles in a lively splash.
Chasing monkeys up a tree,
Bouncing laughter wild and free.

With yellow hats upon their heads,
Joking as they land in beds.
Swinging hearts in playful glee,
Nature's jesters, can't you see?

Twirling leaves of vibrant hue,
Dancing lightly, brave and true.
Every twist and every bend,
Happiness is just around the end.

Banana peels make for great slides,
While mischievous squirrels take their rides.
In this jolly, sunny shroud,
Laughter rings, oh so loud!

Harmony of Yellow and Green

In the whisper of the breeze,
Worlds collide among the trees.
Yellow laughs with vibrant green,
Creating tales that seldom seen.

Frogs in bow ties leap around,
Chanting songs with silly sound.
Each fruit tells a funny story,
Glistening in their fruity glory.

The sun peeks through the leafy dance,
Bouncing shadows in a chance.
Nature's comedy unfolds sweet,
With every joggle, every beat.

Squirrels steal the evening snack,
As critters play their playful hack.
Bumbling bees join in the fun,
With buzz and jig, they spin and run!

Treasures of the Forgotten Fruit

Underneath the leafy crown,
Lies a treasure—golden brown.
Whispers of a hidden prize,
Laughing at the curious eyes.

Wobbling bears in a fruit parade,
Juggling snacks that never fade.
An orange cat joins in the spree,
Chasing shadows, oh so free.

A lizard dons a tiny hat,
Dancing amidst the chatty chat.
Mischief brews where laughter grows,
In this land of yellow shows.

Forgotten fruit becomes the star,
Promising joy near and far.
With each bite, a giggle springs,
Echoing what the silly sings.

Melody of the Swaying Boughs

Gentle breezes start to sway,
In a funny fruity ballet.
Leaves will chuckle, fruits will jive,
In this dance, we feel alive.

The crows croon a merry tune,
As vines twist and around they swoon.
Banana bunches swing and sway,
Joining in the grand cabaret.

Laughter ripples through the space,
As critters waltz in joyful grace.
With every shake and silly jig,
Nature's fun, both bright and big.

Underneath the dazzling show,
Friendship blossoms, oh so slow.
Fruits and friends in wild delight,
Painting shadows, day and night.

A Dance of Yellow Dreams

In a land where laughter grows,
Bright fruits sway with silly toes.
Chasing tales of weighty bliss,
With every slip, how can we miss?

Banish thoughts of being meek,
These curvy snacks just love to peek.
They twirl and toss, a fruity scheme,
In this whimsical yellow dream.

Jokes on each peel that falls,
As monkeys giggle, heed their calls.
A feast so funny, no doubt about,
Where every laugh is what it's about.

So join this frolic, take a chance,
With bouncy feasts, they'll make you dance.
With playful smiles we'll all convene,
In this orchard full of glee and green.

Beneath the Boughs of Bliss

Under arches, deep in glee,
Laughter echoes, wild and free.
Fruits hang low, like giggling sprites,
Dancing shadows on sunny nights.

Bouncing cheeks and silly quirks,
Gather 'round for fruity perks.
With every munch, a fable plays,
In this land where joy displays.

Tangles of vines and blushing cheer,
Ticklish whispers, come draw near.
The beans get cracking, laughter swirls,
In this place, fun unfurls.

So eat and chuckle, take a bite,
Beneath the leaves, all feels right.
In this haven where spirits lift,
The sweetest punchline is the gift.

Secrets of the Orchard

Hidden jokes in leafy hue,
Fruits all giggling, who knew?
Tales of pranks and playful ways,
Whispered underneath the rays.

Curved companions, vibrant and bright,
Chasing shadows in the light.
Silly secrets, ripe and round,
In this twisty plot we've found.

Here's the folly, take a peek,
Fruits conspire, it's blithely sleek.
With every taste, another jest,
It's a game, we know the rest!

So stack the laughs, the fruity fables,
Adventures await at the tables.
With joy and mirth, take a dive,
In this orchard where we thrive.

Radiance in the Rainforest

In a jungle bustling bright,
Fruits aplenty, pure delight.
Chirpy chirps and colors gleam,
Join the feast, let's all redeem.

Bouncing bubbles, laughter blooms,
Underneath the leafy rooms.
Peels do flip and giggles sprout,
As we dance and twist about.

The air is thick with funny beats,
Wiggly vines and leafy treats.
Let's share a chuckle, take your stand,
In this warm, enchanted land.

With every chomp, a riot grows,
In the rainforest, joy overflows.
Let's toast to fun, so bright and grand,
With fruits that dance, all hand in hand.

Bananas in the Moonlight

Under the stars, bananas sway,
Wiggling their peels in a funny display.
A monkey in shades starts to dance,
He thinks it's his very last chance.

Bananas giggle, taking their stand,
Juggling their bunches, a fruity band.
The moonlight chuckles, soft and bright,
As bananas groove through the silly night.

Midnight snacks with a twist of fate,
Slipping on peels, oh, isn't it great?
Laughter echoes in the midnight air,
With bananas swinging, without a care.

In this moonlit world, all's so absurd,
Bananas can't stop their silly word.
They toast to the night with a fruity cheer,
Promising fun every time they appear.

Dappled Light on Soft Skin

In a sunny nook where the shadows tease,
Bananas chuckle in the warm breeze.
Soft skin glitters with dappled light,
A fruity party, oh what a sight!

With squishy cushions beneath our backs,
We share wild stories, no need for facts.
Bananas boasting, oh, what a scene,
They claim they're the stars of the picnic routine.

The sun winks down, a playful spy,
While bananas ponder about pie in the sky.
A fruity debate starts to unfold,
Who's the best snack? Oh, the stories told!

Laughter erupts under trees so green,
With silly antics that can't be seen.
As dappled light dances on our skin,
The fun never stops, let the games begin!

Conversations in a Leafy Sanctuary

In a leafy patch where gossip flows,
Bananas gossip in a row, each knows.
They chat about smoothies, oh, what a blend,
Making wild schemes that never quite end.

One banana slips, a humorous fall,
The others erupt in laughter, all in all.
They banter and giggle, a silly crew,
Life's too short not to join in the fun, too.

With leaves as hats, they play dress up,
Pretending to sip from a coconut cup.
Each chat turns wild; it's pure delight,
In this sanctuary, everything's right.

Conversations twist like a playful vine,
Each story sweeter, just like their brine.
Surrounded by friends in this leafy spree,
Bananas laughing, as happy as can be.

Nectar from the Heart of Summer

In the heart of summer, laughter flows,
Bananas sip nectar, as the warm wind blows.
With sunny smiles and juiciness so bright,
Their fruity humor dances in the light.

Each banana tale is a juicy delight,
Swapping their secrets under the sunlight.
They joke about squirrels and their nutty schemes,
While dreaming of pies in their banana dreams.

Honeybees buzz, joining the fun,
Their sweet little dance makes the day run.
Bananas chuckle at the buzzing crowd,
Creating a party that's cheerful and loud.

In the summer's warmth, friendships ignite,
With laughter and nectar, oh what a sight!
A fruity fiesta with smiles galore,
Nectar dripping, they always ask for more.

Arc of Abundance

In a world of yellow cheer,
Where fruit hangs oh so near,
Monkeys dance and slip about,
Sharing laughs with joyous shouts.

Peeling laughter fills the air,
As critters prance without a care,
Bunches sway in gentle breeze,
Tickling feet with playful tease.

Cracks and giggles, what a sight,
Banana peels, a comical flight,
Rolling down in silly haste,
Chasing slips, we laugh and chase.

Joy and laughter, ripe and bright,
In the grove, everything feels right,
Where the funny fruit grows free,
Stellar spots of glee we see.

The Golden Canopy

Underneath the leafy shade,
Golden fruits with jokes are laid,
Critters whisper quirky tales,
Bouncing vuvezelas, joyous wails.

Squirrels juggling in the sun,
Telling puns 'til day is done,
Even birds drop witty lines,
In this grove where laughter shines.

A slide of peel, a pratfall true,
Animals giggle, join the crew,
Rolling laughter echoes wide,
With every slip, we laugh outside.

Lemon zest, oh what a beat,
In this place, peachy and sweet,
Friends unite in jovial sway,
Singing songs in bright array.

Serenade in a Sunny Glade

In a glade where sunbeams play,
Bananas burst in bright array,
Frisky critters sing along,
To the nature of a lively song.

Swaying branches, giggles loud,
Fruits in clusters, rich and proud,
Bouncing laughter as they land,
Topsy-turvy, all so grand.

With a slip, the mishaps fly,
Twists and tumbles, oh my, oh my!
Through the grove, a dance so free,
Filled with joy and jubilee.

In this sunny serenade,
Every joke a masquerade,
Chasing shadows, we all prance,
In this fruity, fun-filled dance.

The Flavorful Tale

Once upon a curling peel,
Laughter burst like a great meal,
Fruits with names sung loudly here,
As mixed with giggles, brings good cheer.

A bunch of friends, all in a whirl,
Joking round, watch me twirl,
Monkeys mimic with perfect flair,
Life is funny, beyond compare.

Over ripe, they leap and glide,
In this slice of joy, we bide,
Chasing riddles, funny and bright,
The flavor of fun, in pure delight.

As they tumble, one by one,
In the orchard, laughter spun,
Tales of flavors, strong and sweet,
In this grove, our hearts retreat.

Treasures in the Tropics

In a land where yellow fruits hang low,
Monkeys dance and laughter flows.
With hats too big and shoes unmatched,
They gather 'round, oh what a batch!

A parrot squawks with flair and pride,
While sloths take selfies, they can't hide.
The breeze brings tales of laughter loud,
In this quirky, silly, sunlit crowd.

A pirate ship sails by with glee,
Searching for treasure, or maybe tea?
With a map that's drawn on a banana leaf,
They laugh at the spoils—oh, what a relief!

The sun sets low, all giggles cease,
As dreams of fruit begin to fleece.
Tomorrow waits, a day anew,
For more shenanigans, just for you.

Emotions in the Ether

In the whispering breeze, a chuckle's heard,
A million jokes, not one absurd.
With each yellow curve that glistens bright,
They share their secrets, pure delight.

Raindrops tickle, leaves start to sway,
While critters scamper, ready to play.
Confetti of pollen floats on air,
As butterflies giggle in a joyful flare.

A grand parade of fruit parade cheer,
Each weary traveler waves and jeers.
Who knew a harvest could bring such fun?
A sunbeam winked, the day was won!

Even the roots laugh underground,
In this funny land where joy is found.
With each turn and twist, they embrace the jest,
And take a moment, welcome the rest.

Chronicles of the Leafy Veil

A leafy world where giggles grow,
Lurking beneath a laughter show.
The green brigade in shades of lime,
Cracking jokes like it's their time!

Critters stacked in a wobbly tower,
A sight so silly, it's got power.
Chasing dreams with feathery wings,
They laugh at the chaos each wild night brings.

With pots of gold beneath the trees,
They dance on air, breeze on knees.
What treasures lie in this leafy land?
A punchline saved by a furry hand!

As dusk rolls in, shadows play tricks,
Banana bottoms, playful flicks.
The fun persists, no end in sight,
In the chronicles of giggles, pure delight.

Ballet of the Blooms

Amidst the foliage, a show unfolds,
With blooms and giggles daringly bold.
Frogs in tutus leap with grace,
While crickets lead the merry pace.

Petals pirouette in the gentle breeze,
As pollen dancers glide with ease.
A firefly winks like a star on cue,
While flowers chuckle, "We're fabulous too!"

The wind brings music, a happy tune,
As buds bounce lightly, none immune.
With every twirl and spin, they cheer,
In this ballet, there's nothing to fear.

As night wraps the stage in a velvet hue,
The blooms take a bow, a vibrant crew.
With laughter echoing, dreams take flight,
In this blooming ballet, all feels right.

A Symphony of Fruity Aromas

In a land where yellow dreams grow wide,
Laughter dances on the breeze's tide.
With slips and trips, the fun begins,
As monkeys join in, with cheeky grins.

Wiggly worms wear tiny hats,
Organizing a party with acrobatic bats.
Fruit-filled carts roll down the lane,
Who knew veggies could bring such strain?

Chatter fills the air with glee,
Bouncing fruits hide behind a tree.
Each little scoop, a scoop of cheer,
Bananas play hide and seek, oh dear!

So come one, come all, let's skip and sway,
In this quirky patch of green ballet.
With every peel, a joke unfurls,
In this fruity realm, joy twirls!

Shadows of the Climbing Vines

Vines twist and twirl, a wobbly show,
They stretch and bend like a limbo pro.
Laughing leaves tickle the ground,
While roots play peek-a-boo all around.

A sudden slip, a fruit takes flight,
Who knew a launch could bring delight?
Giggling fans cheer from afar,
As a bunch of bananas lands in the car!

Shadow puppets flaunt their flair,
As leaves whisper secrets in the air.
With every gust, a giggle shared,
Those climbing vines are quite prepared!

So tread lightly on this fruity lane,
Where shadows frolic and jokes explain.
When nature plays, nothing feels plain,
In this vibrant world, joy is the gain!

Harvesting Joy from Nature's Bounty

Each harvest day begins with cheer,
With a basket ready, let's shift into gear.
The fruits all chime with silly tunes,
Under the watch of chuckling moons.

Caramel rains and sticky pies,
Nutty squirrels wear their best disguise.
A playful dance of ants and bees,
Silently laughing 'neath leafy trees.

Picking laughter with every bite,
There's no such thing as fruit too ripe!
Bananas giggle in the sun's embrace,
Mischievous hearts steal the race.

So harness joy with your hands and heart,
In this merry market, let's all take part!
Nature's bounty, pretty and bright,
Makes everyday dull days ignite!

The Sway of Sunlit Branches

Golden branches bend and sway,
Singing songs of a bright-filled day.
Beneath the shade, we laugh and play,
Chasing dreams in a fruit buffet.

One branch winks, another shakes,
As giggles rise like frosted flakes.
A fruit falls, hops, and rolls like a ball,
While silly ants parade in thrall.

Sunlit smiles drape every leaf,
Turning harvest into pure belief.
Let's swing from vines, let dreams entwine,
As we dance with joy on this fruity line!

With every color and every hue,
The apples and bananas join the crew.
In this sunny dance where glee is the key,
Branches sway, and life's carefree!

Vibrant Whispers of Nature

In a jungle where giggles bloom,
The monkeys play and sing in tune.
Leaves dance lightly in the breeze,
Tickling toes beneath the trees.

Banana peels, oh what a sight,
Slipping shoes with pure delight.
Laughter echoes near and far,
As critters bump, a wild bazaar.

Creatures plotting fun-filled schemes,
Chasing dreams and ripe regimes.
In every nook, a comical tale,
Where nature hosts its raucous trail.

Clusters sway in jolly cheer,
Fruit-laden joy makes life sincere.
With every chime from quirky ferns,
The heart of nature brightly yearns.

Adventures in the Arc of Growth

Among the giants with leafy crowns,
Silly squirrels wear nutty gowns.
A parrot yells a jolly joke,
As sneaky roots begin to poke.

Wiggly worms with giggles sprout,
Beneath the ground where dreams run out.
They scheme to stretch their squiggly lanes,
To tickle toes of all terrains.

A chubby frog jumps from his throne,
Into a puddle, fully grown.
The splash sends fish into a spin,
In this madcap world, joy wins again.

Blossoms twirl in vibrant grace,
As laughter dances through the space.
In every corner, twists unfold,
In this grand tale of green and gold.

Festivity in the Foliage

Underneath the leafy shade,
Party critters, unafraid.
With the beat of nature's song,
They shimmy, giggle all day long.

Caterpillars wear fancy shoes,
While ants tap dance without a bruise.
The air is thick with jolly vibes,
As laughter flows in neon tribes.

In the branches, draped in cheer,
A raucous crowd, with no fear.
Bouncing jokes from tree to tree,
Nature's satire, wild and free.

Each petal sways, a silly dance,
Life's craziness, a bright expanse.
So join the frolic, sing anew,
In the embrace of greenish hue.

Clusters of Morning Light

Golden rays in playful streams,
Kissing leaves where laughter beams.
Cheeky critters rise with glee,
As dawn unlocks their jubilee.

Fluffy bunnies bounce and roll,
Chasing dreams, they reach their goal.
In soft embraces, joy ignites,
Their antics fill the sunlit heights.

Each fruity friend wears giddy smiles,
Trading winks across the miles.
A whimsical parade unfolds,
In this sunlit world, pure joy beholds.

As daylight dances, hearts align,
In every nook, a giggling shrine.
With nature's humor shining bright,
Morning brings a spark of light.

Echoes of Eden

In a land where monkeys dance and play,
Bananas hang with a bright bouquet,
Laughter echoes through the sunny lanes,
As critters jive on sweet refrains.

A squirrel dons a tiny hat,
Tripping over, then a somersault splat!
The parrots squawk their loud decree,
'Join our party, come swing with me!'

Beneath the branches, we find delight,
Chasing shadows in the fading light,
The fruit of joy, so ripe and bright,
Bringing giggles till the night.

With every slip and every fall,
A tale of clumsiness we recall,
In this paradise of sunny cheer,
The hilarity is always near.

Juicy Chronicles

In a patch where laughter grows so loud,
Bouncing bubbles in the silly crowd,
Watch out for that peckish grouch,
He's spinning tales upon the couch!

A walrus with a fruit hat tall,
Rolls down the hill, giving all a call,
'Mangoes, melons, and oranges here,
But bananas, my friends, that's the real cheer!'

The sloths are having a race today,
Who'll be the last to not delay?
With every 'thud' and 'whoopsie-daisy',
We giggle through the grumpy crazy!

Swinging high on vines of glee,
The wise old owl joins the spree,
With fruity jokes and zany rhymes,
We relish in our fruity crimes.

Pathways of Promise

Down the path where giggles roam,
Each fruit is sweeter than your home,
Bursting flavors of the sunny fate,
Where dancing squirrels initiate.

Here come the ants with a cart so grand,
Bearing snacks that are in high demand,
Banana splits and fruity pies,
Underneath the big blue skies.

A sneaky snake plays hide and seek,
With the laughter loud and the spirits peak,
Be careful where you take a seat,
The bench is sticky with fruity treat!

Our secret paths are full of fun,
With every twist, we break and run,
In this quirky land, we all feel fine,
Every day is like sunshine wine.

Beneath the Gilded Veil

In the shade where shadows play,
We munch and giggle through the day,
With silly voices and radiant smiles,
Our fruity mischief stretches miles.

A monkey juggles in a tree so high,
Dropping fruits that bounce nearby,
A comical show of slipping fate,
Making laughter feel so great!

The iguanas dance in a line with pride,
Wiggling tails and eyes open wide,
As we cheer them from our leafy throne,
Together we share this wild zone.

In every nook and quirky space,
There's a table set for joy and grace,
With wobbly chairs a tad too small,
Join the feast, we'll eat it all!

Ripened Secrets of the Orchard

In green attire, they sway and dance,
A fruity fiesta, a monkey's prance.
Peels slip and slide with cheerful glee,
Who knew fruit could be so free?

Lurking critters with sneaky smiles,
Sneak a snack, then run for miles.
The juiciest laughs are hidden away,
Under leafy roofs where monkeys play.

Sun-kissed treasure, golden and bright,
Makes the jungle feel just right.
With giggles and shouts, they share their prize,
As birds gather 'round for the tasty surprise.

In this orchard where secrets reside,
Joyful antics we cannot hide.
Let's peel back layers, giggles unfurl,
In this fruity world, laughter's the pearl.

Golden Curves in the Jungle

Round and yellow, they reign supreme,
Bouncing like balls in a silly dream.
Jungle critters join in the chase,
Wobbling wonders, a merry race.

Laughter echoes, a playful sound,
As creatures tumble all around.
Slip and slide, they take a fall,
With silly giggles, they have a ball.

Twirling around on a leafy stage,
Fruits of joy, a playful gauge.
Monkeys chuckle, parrots tune,
In the warm embrace of a golden noon.

Loops and curves beneath the trees,
Dancing shadows in the breeze.
A fruit-filled dance, a merry spree,
In the jungle's heart, forever free.

Whispering Leaves of Sunlight

In the sun's arms, they bask in cheer,
Whispers of laughter drift close and near.
Gold smiles peek from leaf to leaf,
In this merry place, there's no grief.

Tiny critters scamper about,
With mischievous giggles and tiny shouts.
They play hide-and-seek in the foliage tight,
A raucous party from morning to night.

Breezes carry secrets, sweet and bright,
While bubbles of joy float into sight.
Each rustle and shake in the verdant sea,
Tells tales of fun, wild and free.

Sunlit laughter weaves through the air,
Jungle's jubilation and moments rare.
A chorus of chuckles, so pure and right,
Where whispers of sunlight take joyful flight.

Echoes Among the Tropic Canopy

Under the canopy, secrets spill,
With ripened fruit, they fit the bill.
Hilarious echoes bounce and thrive,
In the jungle, where silliness comes alive.

Swinging vines and bushy tails,
Ticklish moments and giggling trails.
The laughter grows louder, a playful throng,
As critters jam to a fruity song.

Chasing each other, they tumble down,
Crowned by bananas, a fruity crown.
With every slip, a chorus of mirth,
Jubilant glee fills the earth.

Among the leaves, joy's the decree,
An orchard bursting with jubilee.
The echoes of laughter that flood the land,
Where golden curves meet the playful band.

Splendor of the Tropics

Bright yellow peels on trees so tall,
Swinging squirrels that never fall.
Monkeys giggle, with mischief in hand,
Juggling fruit, just as they planned.

Coconut drinks with a quirky twist,
Who could resist such a fruity kiss?
Parrots squawk in a colorful display,
While frogs croak jokes all through the day.

An iguana struts, looking so fine,
Claiming the crown of the fruity vine.
But little does he know, oh dear,
He's wearing a hat made of banana peel!

Under the sun, the laughter does grow,
As every creature steals the show.
In this sweet land of joy and cheer,
We dance with fruit, year after year!

Laughter Amongst the Leaves

Leaves whisper secrets, a ticklish breeze,
Where monkeys wear ties and beg for cheese.
A parrot's joke, sharp as a knife,
Turns the jungle into comedy life.

Slapstick antics with every swing,
As funny fruits begin to sing.
A pineapple slips on a mango's skin,
And we all burst out laughing within.

An old tortoise with his slow pace,
Tells tales of the wild with such grace.
But watch out for the slippery patch,
Where laughter erupts with every scratch!

Under the canopy, a circus awaits,
With giggles and chuckles, it celebrates.
A world so silly, you can't help but grin,
Where joy grows wild, and fun will win!

Sunlit Sanctuary

Golden hues light up the scene,
Where fruit-frogs bounce, oh so keen.
Sunshine beams on a cheeky crowd,
Swinging and swaying, so bold and loud.

In the shade of palms, a dance-off starts,
Each creature flaunts their funny arts.
With bananas held high like trophies in hand,
Every moment feels perfectly planned.

The laughter bubbles like a sweet soda,
Echoing tales of the nearby moda.
A lizard in shades, oh what a sight,
Dancing to tunes from morning till night.

Beneath the gleam of the bright blue sky,
Every giggle and snicker will fly.
In this sunlit haven, fun never fades,
Here joy blooms wild in playful cascades!

Dappled Shadows of Delight

In dappled light, the fun takes flight,
As critters gather with pure delight.
Silly antics and whispering leaves,
Hide the laughter that everyone weaves.

Chattering monkeys tie knots in vines,
Making hats from fruity designs.
A duck wears one, and a goat must cheer,
As laughter echoes, sincere and clear.

Squirrels compete in a zany race,
Through branches and leaves, they make their pace.
But the prize is won by a clever old snail,
With a twinkle of mischief in his trail.

As shadows dance on this playful ground,
Joy is the treasure that we have found.
In this comedic realm, we forever play,
Woven together in funny ballet!